When were you born? Were you born in a hospital or elsewhere, What's the story?

What is your full name and why were you named that?

Are you named after anyone, or do you know the reason why your parents gave you the names that they did?

____

____

____

____

Did you have a nickname that your siblings or friends call you? How did you get the nickname?

____

____

____

____

Did you ever hear any stories about anything interesting that happened during or soon after your birth?

What were the full names and places of
birth of your parents and grandparents?

Parents
____

____

____

____

____

Grandparents
____

____

____

____

____

Could you tell me a story or a special memory about your parents and grandparents?

<u>Parents</u>

Grandparents

How many children were in your family?
What are there full names?

Could you tell me a story or a special memory about your brothers and sisters?

How did your family spend time together when you were young?

Did you ever have a Family game night?

____

____

If so, what games would your family play?

____

____

____

____

____

____

____

____

What kind of car(s) did your family have
when you were growing up?

____

____

____

____

____

How were those cars different from the
cars today?

____

____

____

____

____

What would you and your family do when
the electricity in your house went out,
when you were a child?

____

____

____

____

____

Did your household always have a
television?

____

____

If no, when did your family get their first
television?

____

____

Was your first television a black and white set, or a color set

____

____

What shows did your family watch on television?

____

____

____

____

____

____

____

____

What was your favorite show to watch on television?

____

____

Did your family ever take vacations together?

____

____

____

What was your favorite vacation that your family ever took?

____

____

____

____

How often did your parents read to you?

____

____

____

Did you ever play any tricks or pranks on your parents or siblings?

____

____

____

____

____

____

____

How did your parents discipline you?

____

____

____

____

____

____

____

Did your family ever home-make any clothing?

____

____

____

If your family bought clothing from a store, which store(s) did your family buy clothing from?

____

____

____

____

____

On what occasions would you get new clothing or new outfits?

____

____

____

____

How often would your parents take you to get new shoes?

____

____

____

____

____

How would you dress, as a child?

____

____

____

____

____

Who would baby sit you when your parents weren't home?

____

____

____

____

____

Who was your favorite baby sitter?
And why?

____

____

____

____

____

Can you tell me about our family history,
And the family tree?

What do you appreciate most about your parents?

What is the earliest memory that you have?

Who was your childhood best friend?

____

____

What is diferent about growing up today
than when you were a child?

____

____

____

____

____

____

____

____

____

What is the most surprising thing you enjoy about being a child?

____

____

____

____

____

____

____

Did your family move often, during your childhood?

____

____

____

____

Did you like or dislike moving?

____

____

____

Can you remember all the different places
you lived, and what years or dates you
moved?

____

____

____

____

____

____

____

Did you have a bed time?

If so, what time did you have to be in bed by?

How old were you when this bed time was enforced?

What was your favorite movie you ever saw in your childhood?

Do you remember what was the first movie you ever saw?

____

____

How often did you see movies at the theater, as a child?

____

____

How much did movie tickets cost, when you were little?

____

____

When did you learn how to swim? Where did you go swimming as a child?

____

____

____

____

Did you ever go fishing or hunting, as a child child?

____

____

____

____

Do you remember the day when you learned how to ride a bicycle?

____

____

How did you learn how to ride a bicycle? Did anyone help you?

____

____

____

____

Did you like to read books, as a child?

How often would you read?

What was your favorite book to read, as a child

Did you ever run away or hide from your
parents after you had done something
wrong?

Did you ever get into a physical fight with another child?

What was the worst injury you ever got, as a child?

How did your parents react on the injury?

What was the angriest you ever got, as a
child?

____

____

____

____

____

What is your saddest memory from
childhood?

____

____

____

____

____

What is your happiest memory from childhood?

____

____

____

____

____

What is your scariest memory from childhood?

____

____

____

____

____

What was the one thing you were always most scared of, as a child?

____

____

____

____

____

Do you remember any particularly frightening nightmares you had as a child?

____

____

____

____

____

What are some of your most memorable dreams that you had as a child, either scary or non-scary?

What is something that you were just
never able to understand, as a child?

____

____

____

____

____

____

What is the funniest thing you ever
remember saying, as a small child?

____

____

____

____

____

What is something that you were just never able to understand, as a child?

____

____

____

____

____

____

What is the funniest thing you ever remember saying, as a small child?

____

____

____

____

____

How did you celebrate birthdays in your family?

____

____

____

____

____

____

What was your favorite or most memorable birthday gift you ever received, as a child?

____

____

____

____

____

What was your least favorite type of
birthday gift to receive, when you were little?

____

____

____

____

____

____

How did you celebrate Thanksgiving in
your family?

____

____

____

____

____

How did you cebrate on Christmas day in your family?

How did you celebrate on New years'
Day in your family?

____

____

____

____

____

____

Were there any holidays that your family
celebrated when you were growing up,
which most other people don't celebrate?

____

If so, what were they and how were they
celebrated?

____

____

What was the first school you attended?

____

____

Who was the coolest or most popular kid in your class?

____

____

____

____

Why were they so cool or popular?

____

____

____

____

____

What were your favorite subjects in grade/
Key stage school?

____

____

____

____

____

____

Did you play any junior sports in grade/
Key stage school?

____

____

____

____

____

Did you play any musical Instruments in a band during grade/ Key stage school?

____

If so, which ones?

____

____

____

____

If you were in a school band, what songs that you played in your school band do you remember the best, or which songs were your favorites to play?

____

____

____

____

Did any of your siblings or cousins go to
school with you?

____

____

____

If you had siblings or cousins that went to
school with you, what classes or school
activities did you participate in with them

____

____

____

____

____

____

____

What was one of your favorite class field
trips that you took?

Where did you sit in classroom?
And why?

Were you ever disciplined by a teacher or sent to the principal's office?

If so, what happened?

How often was your school delayed or cancelled due to snow or other inclement weather?

____

____

Were you ever prevented from getting to school because of snowy roads or flooded roads?

____

____

____

____

____

____

____

____

Were there any subjects or teachers you
disliked particularly liked or disliked? Why?

____

____

____

____

____

Who was your best friend in high school ?

____

____

____

____

____

How would people who knew you in high school describe you?

Did you work during high school ? If so, What did you do? If not Why didnt you ?

What did you do after high school ?

Where was the farthest away from home that
you ever traveled, before your 18th birthday

____

____

____

____

____

How were your next door neighbors like?
friendly, mean, sociable, etc?

____

____

____

____

____

How old were your next door neighbors ?

____

____

____

____

How often did your family or next door
neighbors visit each other ?

____

____

____

____

____

Did you ever get troubles as a child or teenager? Did you have a curfew and what time was it ? Did you ever miss curfew ?

Did you ever have low points as a teenager?
How did you get through it ?

Tell me about a leader who impacted your life for good when you were a teenager ?

____

____

____

____

____

____

____

____

____

____

____

Who were your friends from school what did
you do together for fun ?

Did you do any sports or clubs when you were a teen? If so what are your favorite memories ?

Do you remember any words or sayings that were common in your youth that nobody says anymore or very rare ?

What was the biggest thing you ever got in trouble for ?

What pet have you had ? Tell me more about them

What is your favorite place you have ever visited and how was it like ?

What is the longest trip that you have ever gone on ? Where did you go ?

What is the most beautiful place you have ever visited and what was it like ?

How did you fall in love ?

____

____

____

____

____

____

____

____

How old were you when you fell in love ?

____

____

____

How many times have you been in love ?

____

____

____

____

Who was your first date? How long did you date?

____

____

____

____

____

____

How did you meet my mum/ dad / Grandma/
Grandpa? Tell me more about that?

How did you know that it was the "real deal" ?

How often did you go for dates? How was it like ?

What advise do you have on love and
marriage for couples today ?

Where was the first place you lived away from home? Do you have any crazy roommates stories?

What is the best christmas or birthday gift you
have ever recieved and given?

____

____

____

What is your favorite thing to do on the
weekends?

____

____

____

____

____

____

____

Did you ever get really sick or have to go the hospital? What happened?

What was your first job?

____

____

____

____

What was your first car you drove?

____

____

____

Where was your first home out of your
parents house?

____

____

____

What or who was your favorite ?

Color ?

____

Cookie ?

____

Drink ?

____

Flavor of ice cream ?

____

Flower ?

____

Fruit ?

____

Holiday ?

____

What or who was your favorite ?

Meal ?

____

Movie star ?

____

Movie ?

____

Musical group ?

____

Musical instrument ?

____

Painting ?

____

Poem ?

____

What or who was your favorite ?

Animal ?

Athlete ?

Author ?

Board game ?

Book ?

Candy ?

Card game ?

What or who was your favorite ?

Poet ?

____

Restaurant ?

____

Season ?

____

Singer ?

____

Song ?

____

Sport ?

____

Style of music ?

____

If you had to pick a label for your family members (mother, father, brothers, sisters....) Who fits each of the following descriptions during your childhood ?

Best cook

____

Best gardener

____

____

Best house keeper

____

____

Best looking

____

Best memory

____

If you had to pick a label for your family members (mother, father, brothers, sisters....) Who fits each of the following descriptions during your childhood ?

Calmest

____

Hardest worker

____

____

Biggest tease

____

____

Funniest

____

Best story teller

____

____

If you had to pick a label for your family members (mother, father, brothers, sisters....) Who fits each of the following descriptions during your childhood ?

Most athletic

____

Most colorful

____

____

Most frugal

____

____

Most sociable

____

Most creative

____

____

If you had to pick a label for your family members (mother, father, brothers, sisters....) Who fits each of the following descriptions during your childhood ?

Most generous

____

Most political active

____

____

Shortest

____

____

Tallest

____

Quietest

____

____

What are your top five best memories?

What lessons would you like me to learn from
your experiences growing up?

____

____

____

____

____

____

____

____

____

____

____

Notes

Notes

Notes

Notes

Notes

Notes

Notes

Notes